DATE DUE

OCT 1 9 1995	JUN 0 3 2003	
NOV 0 3 1995	JUL 1 8 2003 2/4/04	
NOV 2 5 1995	NOV 0 3 2004	
MAR 1 8 1996	3/30/05	
MAY 1 6 1996		
MAR 0 6 1997		
APR 0 7 1997		
MAY 1 3 1997		
MAY 0 9 1998		
SEP 1 0 1998		
NOV 1 6 1998		
DEC 2 8 1998		
JAN 0 9 1999		
MAR 0 1 1999		
MAY 0 7 1999		
FEB 0 4 2000		
OCT 1 2 2001		
GAYLORD		PRINTED IN U.S.A.

PLANETS

SOLAR SYSTEM

Lynda Sorensen

The Rourke Corporation, Inc.
Vero Beach, Florida 32964

Edited by Sandra A. Robinson

PHOTO CREDITS
All photos courtesy of NASA

Library of Congress Cataloging-in-Publication Data
Sorensen, Lynda, 1953-
   Planets / by Lynda Sorensen.
      p. cm. — (The Solar system)
   Includes index.
   Summary: Photographs and simple text present information about the nine planets of our solar system.
   ISBN 0-86593-274-3
   1. Planets—Juvenile literature. [1. Planets. 2. Solar system.]
I. Title. II. Series: Solar system (Vero Beach, Fla.)
QB602.S67 1993
523.4—dc20   93-14874
                                        CIP
                                         AC

Printed in the USA

TABLE OF CONTENTS

THE PLANETS

The nine largest objects that travel around the sun are planets. Each planet is shaped like a great ball. Our Earth is one of them.

The planets are part of our **solar system.** The solar system includes the sun, planets and many smaller objects, such as moons and **asteroids,** or "minor planets."

The planets move in circular paths, called orbits, around the sun. The sun is our nearest star. Unlike the sun, planets do not produce their own heat and light.

Planets orbit around the sun,
the center of our solar system

INNER AND OUTER PLANETS

The four planets closest to the sun—Mercury, Venus, Earth and Mars—are called the "inner" planets. They have land—a solid surface. Inner planets are the warmest planets because they are closest to the sun's heat.

Four of the "outer" planets—Jupiter, Saturn, Uranus and Neptune—are large, cold, spinning globes made mostly of gas.

Scientists know little about Pluto because it is so distant. Pluto was not even discovered by scientists until 1930.

Jupiter, the largest of the planets, is a cold, spinning globe of gas

PLANET EARTH

Planet Earth is the third planet from the sun, which is 93 million miles away. Earth is the fifth largest planet in our solar system.

As far as anyone knows, Earth is the only planet with life. It is the only planet with oceans, and air that humans can breathe. It is also the only planet that is not named for a Greek or Roman god.

All planets receive heat and light from the sun. Earth receives just the right amount to support life.

Australia and a portion of planet Earth are shown in this photograph from a spacecraft

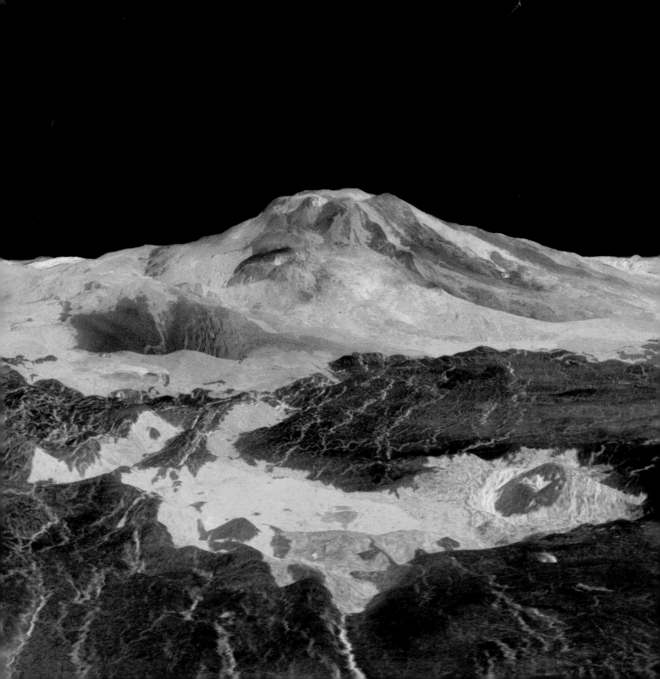

MERCURY AND VENUS

Mercury is the planet closest to the sun. The eighth largest planet, Mercury is flaming hot where it faces the sun.

Mercury's surface is covered with dents, or craters.

Venus is the second planet from the sun, but it is probably the hottest planet. Venus is covered by thick clouds that trap heat, producing temperatures that will melt lead!

Venus travels around the sun once in 225 days, compared to Mercury's 88-day trip.

The rugged surface of Venus and the volcano Sapas Mons were photographed in 1992 by the Magellan spacecraft

Jupiter (upper left) and four of its 16 moons

*A close-up view of Saturn's colorful, distinctive rings,
photographed from the Voyager 2 spacecraft*

MARS AND JUPITER

Fourth planet from the sun, the "red planet" Mars travels on the far side of Earth. The rugged surface of Mars is reddish from the rust in its soil.

Mars has two moons, natural bodies that orbit it. Jupiter, the fifth planet from the sun, has 16 moons! Io, one of Jupiter's moons, is the only place other than Earth where erupting volcanoes have been photographed.

Jupiter is the largest planet. Photos of Jupiter's surface reveal the "Great Red Spot," the center of a huge storm that is much larger than Earth.

Jupiter's "Great Red Spot" and one of its moons, Io, are on the right in this photo from Voyager 1

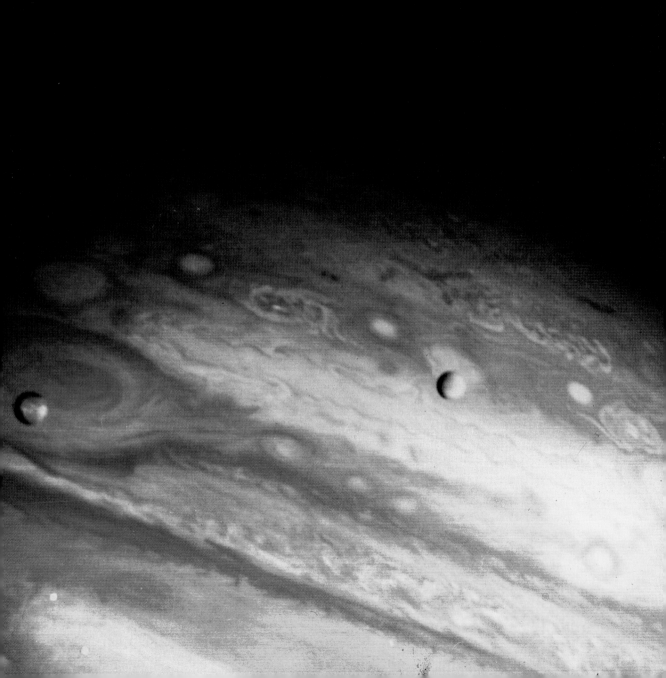

SATURN AND URANUS

Saturn, the sixth planet from the sun, is known for its beautiful rings. The rings are made of pieces of ice or ice-covered rock. Unfortunately, the rings cannot be seen without a **telescope.**

Saturn, the second largest planet, has 18 moons.

Temperatures on Uranus, the seventh planet from the sun, reach 353 degrees below zero Fahrenheit. Fifteen moons orbit Uranus during its long— 84-year—trip around the sun.

Saturn's distinctive rings are shown in this image taken by NASA's Hubble Space Telescope when Saturn was 860 million miles from Earth

NEPTUNE AND PLUTO

Neptune, orbited by eight moons, is the eighth planet form the sun and the fourth largest. It takes this frigid planet 165 Earth years to make just one orbit around the sun, compared to Earth's 365 days (one Earth year).

Mysterious Pluto is the smallest, most distant planet—over 3 billion miles from the sun! At times, Pluto crosses Neptune's orbit and moves closer to the sun than Neptune.

Neptune and Pluto are the only planets that cannot be seen without a telescope.

From its moon Miranda (in front),
the bluish cloudtops of Uranus
and its narrow bands might look
like this to a traveler

ROCKETING TO THE PLANETS

America's National Aeronautics and Space Administration (NASA) and Russia have sent many rockets into space for a closer look at some of the planets in our solar system. Spacecraft have actually landed on Venus and Mars, but not with **astronauts** aboard.

NASA's Viking Mission in 1976 gave scientists a close-up view of Mars. A space robot, called a **lander,** explored a small part of the **Martian** surface. The lander found no signs of life, but conditions on Mars are not too harsh for life of some kind.

The reddish soil of Mars, photographed on the Martian surface by the Viking 1 lander unit

STUDYING THE PLANETS

Astronomers are scientists who study the solar system and other space objects. Astronomers work with telescopes and other scientific instruments in special buildings called **observatories.**

Most observatories are built on mountains, away from lights and polluted air. Some man-made **satellites** in space are also used as observatories.

People can learn more about the planets and stars in a **planetarium.** Using special lights, a planetarium shows programs about the solar system and stars on the inside of a dome.

Glossary

asteroids (AS ter oidz) — rocky objects that travel in orbit around the sun but which sometimes break up after collisions

astronaut (AS trun awt) — a person who travels in space

astronomer (uh STRON uh mer) — a scientist who studies the sun, moon, stars and other heavenly bodies

lander (LAND er) — a special type of robot built to set itself down upon moons and planets

Martian (MAR shun) — having to do with Mars

observatory (uhb ZERV uh tor ee) — a place where astronomers view and study the stars and solar system

planetarium (plan ih TARE ee um) — a place to view special shows about outer space; the instrument that produces such shows

satellite (SAT el ite) — like the moon, any of several fairly large bodies that orbit the planets; a man-made object that is rocketed into orbit

solar system (SO ler SIS tim) — the sun, planets and other heavenly bodies that orbit around the sun

telescope (TEL ess kope) — a powerful instrument used to magnify and view distant objects

INDEX